Blowing Up Balloons

baby poems for parents

Vanessa Proctor
Gregory Piko

Blowing Up Balloons

Text © 2017 Vanessa Proctor & Gregory Piko
Cover art/illustrations © 2017 Vanessa Proctor

ISBN 978-1-936848-78-2

Red Moon Press
PO Box 2461
Winchester VA
22604-1661 USA
www.redmoonpress.com

first printing

for

Tristan & Natalie (V.P.)

and

Benjamin & James (G.P.)

We all delight in the anticipation and joy that comes with the arrival of a new baby. We marvel at baby's every achievement and we are nourished by the sense of fulfilment parenthood provides.

Blowing Up Balloons invites new parents and their families to share and celebrate this amazing journey from the creation of a new life through to early childhood.

Blowing Up Balloons shares the expectation of pregnancy, the euphoria of a birth and the responsibility and satisfaction of raising young children.

Blowing Up Balloons

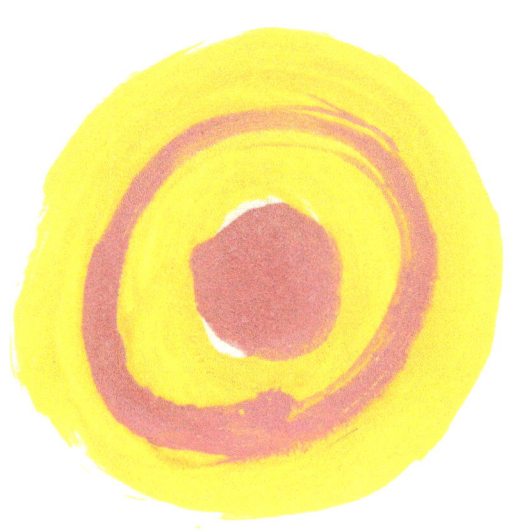

no-one knows
how the world began
tending a seed

indigo sky
choosing a special star
to make my wish

distracted the curve of a new moon

breakfast
throwing up
baby names

grandma's doll
will I ever
have a daughter?

nieces and nephews
broad-brimmed hats
dot the garden

nearly spring—
we stencil daisies
on nursery walls

pregnant
someone knows
when I stumble

so peaceful
inside my womb
Mozart for two

obstetrician's office
a sudden urge
      ...to use the toilet

seven months
my husband asks
for a foot rub

stretchmarks—
proof that you
have changed me

hand on my belly
his fingers
give a little bounce

sleepless night
we pack the hospital bag
again

even the birds
are silent—
a week overdue

all through the night
the sound of rain
on the skylight

wanting
not wanting
this child to be born

around dawn the dinghy breaks its mooring

labour ward
the silence before
baby's first cry

one breath
and then another
      what life brings

a frond uncurls newborn fingers

first light
the steady suck of my son
at my breast

our newborn
perfectly formed
asparagus spear

touching your cheek
the grin
on daddy's face

his little girl
so many shades
of pink

winter dawn
holding my baby
... closer

baby's balloon
floats above the bed ...
were you inside me?

patchwork quilt
the women discuss
stitches

eyes closed
tightly wrapped
unborn again

mid-morning
the midwives share a joke
over cups of tea

leaving hospital
the jacarandas
in full bloom

I wake to check
you're still breathing
first night home

he leans the parenting book
    toward the fairy light

family photos
her tiny feet
                on mummy's
                on daddy's

single mother
feeling sleep come
to her baby

the way sunlight plays
on the change table
his first smile

and yet . . .
only breast milk
went in

grandpa flicks
back your strand of hair
rock 'n' roller

before breakfast
      pacing the streets
            with pram and dog

after the feed
the imprint of your tiny ear
on my arm

her breast against me
the dentist talks
of her baby

fresh celery
trying not to snap
at each other

almost light ...
baby coos mingle
with birdsong

little ray of sunshine
the daughter grandad
never had

a chink of moonlight
across my baby's cheek
evening calm

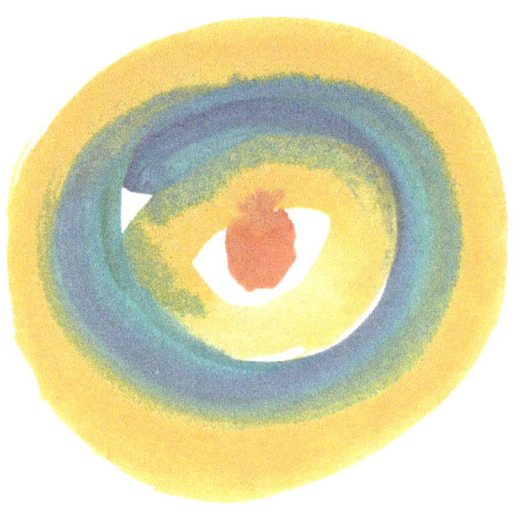

baby and I
without our beanies
almost spring

mother and child
the rhythm of the cat
lapping milk

a patch of drool
      on her christening dress

her grandson's lips
just a little like hers
chinese whispers

tears gush
from my angel's eyes ...
and then a giggle

baby Lily
first visit to the office
since before the birth

how to say no to my friend
        with the weak wrists

she feels no need
to make a statement
modesty shawl

date night
a trace of crème brûlée
in my milk

crying baby
that faraway look
in the dog's eyes

my child stares into
my childhood pond
reflection

mothers' night out
we all head home
at nine

summer afternoon
baby and I discover
the beauty of leaves

mothers' group
the jingle of keys
in little fists

on the phone
      talking daddy through
her first steps

playtime
he posts his toys
through the cat flap

parking ticket
my toddler wants
one too

his teddy bear
stares into space ...
dark matter

her grandson's cheek
the feel of lettering
on a favourite book

finger painting . . .
the easel
a work of art

sailboats bounce
in the ferry's wake—
running after mum

a trip to the park
again we stop at the place
where he lost his balloon

all the kids' clothes
on the bedroom floor
cherry blossoms

heavy rain ...
my son says
listen to the music

dandelions
the toddler
blows a daisy

he holds it up
to hear the sea
shark egg

still the bogong
beats the window
her little tantrum

night terrors
his tiny body
warm against mine

liquidambar
already my toddler's hair
darkening

bedtime story
evening packs away
the autumn colours

my son
blowing up balloons
just to hear them fart

a small cloud
clings to the mountain
first day of school

bellying up
to the boab tree . . .
grandma's embrace

the clearest water
my daughter's made-up song
drifts across the bay

breaking wave
the child gives her ice-cream
a big lick

family dinner
everyone wants to sit next to
the fish tank

eager fingers
the pie crust
            breaks

shoes
in
line
by
the
door

the dog sniffs each pair

bathtime
they re-enact the sinking
of the titanic

the last cupcake
great-grandma shares
a little of her life

fading light
a small boy hurls rocks
at the surf

summer clouds
my children see dinosaurs
in everything

six feet
flopping in puddles
you and puppy

walking home from ballet
my daughter pirouettes
through the blossom

children's voices
from the cherry orchard
   . . . summer dusk

About Haiku

The short poems in this collection take the form of haiku, a style of poetry originating in Japan. Each haiku portrays the beauty of a moment in a way that is personal, allowing the reader to experience the scene and to link the experience with memories of their own.

Many of us in the Western world expect haiku to be written in three lines using a 5-7-5 syllable pattern, however literary haiku written in English do not adhere to this form. English-language haiku best capture the spirit of the original Japanese poems when using fewer than 17 syllables.

For further reading, see:

> www.thehaikufoundation.org
>
> www.australianhaikusociety.org

VANESSA PROCTOR first discovered haiku while living and working in Japan in the early 1990s. She now lives in Sydney, Australia. Vanessa was a founding member of the Australian Haiku Society and has been President of the Society since 2016. Her haiku have been widely published internationally and she has won several awards for her work, including first prize in the New Zealand Poetry Society's 2014 international haiku competition. Her chapbook *Temples of Angkor* was published by Sunline Press in 2003 and her eChapbook *Jacaranda Baby* was published by Snapshot Press in 2012. One of her haiku can be found carved in stone on the Katikati Haiku Pathway in New Zealand.

Vanessa was featured in *A New Resonance 3: Emerging Voices in English-Language Haiku* (Red Moon Press, 2001) and her writing has appeared in several volumes of *The Red Moon Anthology of English-Language Haiku*.

GREGORY PIKO lives in Yass, Australia. He served as Secretary of the Australian Haiku Society from 2010 to 2014. His haiku have been widely published in Australia, the United States, the United Kingdom and other countries. His writing appeared in *Haiku in English: The First Hundred Years* (WW Norton, 2013) and *A Vast Sky: An Anthology of Contemporary World Haiku* (Tancho Press, 2015). He received a 2010 Touchstone Award from The Haiku Foundation (USA) and won first prize in the New Zealand Poetry Society's 2011 international haiku competition. Several of Gregory's haiku are available via *THF Haiku*, The Haiku Foundation's app for the iPhone.

Gregory was featured in *A New Resonance 7: Emerging Voices in English-Language Haiku* (Red Moon Press, 2011) and his writing has appeared in several volumes of *The Red Moon Anthology of English-Language Haiku*.

ACKNOWLEDGEMENTS

Some of the poems in this collection were first published in *Blithe Spirit, Bottle Rockets, Eucalypt, Famous Reporter, Frogpond, Heron's Nest, Ice Diver, Paper Wasp* and *Presence*.